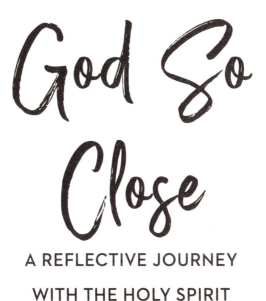

God So Close

A REFLECTIVE JOURNEY
WITH THE HOLY SPIRIT

BECKY THOMPSON

W PUBLISHING GROUP

AN IMPRINT OF THOMAS NELSON

Published in Nashville, Tennessee, by W Publishing, an imprint of Thomas Nelson. W Publishing and Thomas Nelson are registered trademarks of HarperCollins Christian Publishing, Inc.

Thomas Nelson titles may be purchased in bulk for educational, business, fund-raising, or sales promotional use. For information, please email SpecialMarkets@ThomasNelson.com.

The author is represented by Alive Literary Agency, www.aliveliterary.com.

ISBN 978-0-7852-3678-8 (softcover)
ISBN 978-0-7852-9179-4 (eBook)

Library of Congress Control Number: 2021951014

Printed in the United States of America
22 23 24 25 26 LSC 10 9 8 7 6 5 4 3 2 1

CONTENTS

CONTENTS

TO YOU, BEFORE WE BEGIN

Yay! You are here! That's the phrase printed in black ink across the brown welcome mat on my front porch where I live in Oklahoma. If you were to walk up to my door and ring the bell, before I even had a chance to greet you, my welcome mat would let you know that I'm genuinely glad you've come to my home.

Whenever someone opens a book I have written, it feels to me as if they have shown up at my house and we are about to spend some time together. So I'll begin this quick letter to you at the beginning of our journey with the same enthusiastic greeting you'd find if you popped onto my front porch.

Yay! You *are here!*

I realize that we probably have never met. Maybe the only thing you know about me is that my name is printed on the cover of this resource. (If you have read my other works, Hello again! I'm glad you're back! We are going to have fun!) But if you have been invited on this journey by a friend or you stumbled onto these words on your own, I suppose it would be a good idea to introduce myself.

I'm Becky, and I live in Northwest Oklahoma with my

husband, Jared, and our three kids. Jared and I were both raised in Oklahoma, but we spent three and half years in California and Tennessee following God on an adventure of faith. We learned a lot, experienced so much, and made wonderful new friends during those years. We were also deeply grateful that the next steps of His plan for us led us home to our family.

I write books like *God So Close* and others on hope and healing. You'll find me behind my laptop or the wheel of my van most days doing the same things you do. Sure, my schedule and my story might be different from yours, but I promise my days are full of the same stuff you experience—trial and triumph, faith and fear, hope and heartache, and the desire to know God and be known by Him. I have a feeling it wouldn't take us long to find where our stories overlap and all the places where we could nod in agreement and say, "You too? That's how I feel about that as well."

All of this said, I know you're not here to learn about me. Sure, it's a good idea to give you a proper welcome and let you know who is speaking to you, but let's be honest and talk about why you're really here. You're here to discover more about the Holy Spirit. I have a feeling you want more than ordinary.

I can imagine that this guidebook came to be in your possession in one of a number of ways. Perhaps you ordered it online, or you found it in a bookstore. Maybe a group of women you know invited you to go through this material together. Or maybe you're just curious. You saw the title, someone shared something on social media, or you're standing in a bookstore now and haven't even purchased a copy of *God So Close,* but you can't help but wonder, *What is a reflective journey with the Holy Spirit? What is really being offered here?*

Oh, my friend, I believe this journey is what your heart has needed and perhaps you didn't even know it. Sure, you might need joy or peace or a good break from everything that's heavy in your life. I understand. It has been hard, hasn't it? There are so many things you carry and so much you might wish you could put down. What I'm offering you here is the reminder that the only one who can carry it all, take care of what's heavy, and sort through all the details you're trying to untangle on your own is right there in the room with you this moment. He isn't distant or distracted. He's God So Close.

My prayer is that as you read through the book and engage with this material, you'll find opportunities to encounter the Holy Spirit again and again. I don't just mean encounter truths about Him. I mean you will expect to meet with Him as He helps you discover who He is personally, recognize His voice more clearly, and trust that He is leading you so you can follow Him confidently.

Your Invitation to an Interactive Journey with the Holy Spirit

So, what is the process? How is this guidebook best used?

This guidebook has fourteen sections, one for each chapter of *God So Close*. It's my hope that you will read a chapter of the book and then turn to the corresponding pages here in this resource. In each section, you'll find that the theme of each chapter is addressed in a conversational style. You'll be invited to pause and ponder, and then you'll pray and press into His presence.

Let's Pause and Ponder: We will pause and intentionally set aside time to reflect on the text and listen for the Holy Spirit's voice. Then we will look at the questions asked throughout the chapter and explore new points of reflection.

Let's Pray and Press In: We will speak with the Father and thank Him for the revelation of His Holy Spirit. Then we will position our hearts to listen and lean into the presence of the God who comes close and speaks with us.

One thing I want to make sure to mention is that we are all on different parts of our journey with the Holy Spirit. Perhaps the conversations we will have in the pages ahead will serve as a reminder of what you already know and need to remember. On the other hand, the content of this guidebook is possibly brand-new to you, and I want to be clear: that's okay too. The purpose of this process is to bring clarity to the person, work, and power of the Holy Spirit by examining what the Word says is true about Him. So whether you're learning for the first time or your heart is being realigned with what you already knew to be true, this journey is for you.

The Spirit of truth, the Holy Spirit, is drawing us, as daughters of God, back into an understanding of Him in His fullness. He's removing doubt and confusion. And even now, He's preparing our hearts for what will come next. Before we begin, let's pray.

Father,

   We want to know You, to be led by You, and to understand what it means to be full of Your presence. We ask You to remove all confusion in our hearts and minds. Awaken our hearts to Your Spirit. Lead us in love. We ask in Jesus' name. Amen.

CHAPTER 1

THE INVITATION OF THE HOLY SPIRIT

God Wants You to Know Him

I have been starstruck exactly one time in my life. It would make sense for this encounter to have taken place while we were living in Los Angeles and bumping into countless people you'd recognize from your favorite TV shows and movies . . . but no. This event actually took place about ten years prior in Pigeon Forge, Tennessee. Ironic, right?

The weekend of this event, I was speaking at a youth convention on behalf of the Christian university where I worked as the admissions director. I presented information about the programs the university offered to an audience of a few thousand high schoolers. Let's just say I wasn't the person they were eager to hear from that weekend.

At the same convention, popular Christian music artists had been invited to lead worship. These guys were the reason people bought tickets, and they made the weekend worthwhile. I didn't anticipate running into any of them backstage, but when I was given the opportunity to sit down and have a short conversation with one well-known artist, I temporarily lost my ability to make coherent sentences. I did an embarrassing amount of nervous giggling, and to this day, I cringe when I replay those few moments of my life.

Now, I was younger then, which could have something to do with how I responded to meeting this person, but I think my reaction was driven by an emotional connection I had with their songs. The lyrics had encouraged me, uplifted me, and reminded me of important truths about who God is. It was an honor to meet the person who had made a real impact on my life through their work.

I think you and I could come up with a list of people who have made an impact on our lives without having ever met them in person. Maybe it was an author or a person you follow on social media, or maybe it was a musician who penned lyrics that revealed feelings you hadn't been able to articulate. There are people who are a part of our stories, even though we don't know them face-to-face.

I wonder, however, does God ever feel like a person you know much about but perhaps haven't met face-to-face? We believe He is real and good and that the stories about Him are true. We know He works in our lives, and maybe we've even heard His voice and been prompted by Him to take a specific action. Yet, I wonder if you could point to a moment when you were overwhelmed by the reality that the Holy Spirit was in the room and you were meeting this person who made such a big impact on your life. How would you behave if you knew God Himself was in the room?

From the beginning of this journey, it is important for us to remember that our hearts desire a relationship with the Spirit of God, not just an encounter with the idea of God. It's the difference between hearing the songs of the artist and meeting the person who wrote the lyrics face-to-face.

Let's Pause and Ponder

How well do you know the Holy Spirit? I'm not talking about how much you know about Him. I'm asking, how well do you know the Holy Spirit as your friend? Take a moment to be honest about your relationship with Him. (Remember, there is no wrong answer. This is just an opportunity to document here at the beginning how you feel about your relationship.)

_____

_____

_____

_____

Can you point to a moment when you were certain that God was with you and His presence made you awestruck? Perhaps it was an encounter similar to the one I shared in chapter 1, or maybe it was very different. Whether you were by yourself or in a group, in worship or alone driving in your car, take some time to write out your story.

_____

_____

_____

How clearly do you hear the voice of the Holy Spirit? Do you ever feel as though it is difficult to discern His voice? Why or why not? (We will focus on this subject in depth in chapter 9.)

_____

_____

_____

Do you feel as though the Holy Spirit prompts you to take certain actions or make specific choices daily? Monthly? Ever? Take a moment to write out a time you felt led by Him.

_____

_____

_____

God So Close Chapter Questions

As we begin our journey into a deeper understanding of who the Holy Spirit is, let's take a moment to write down who we know Him to be today. When you complete this guidebook, we'll revisit these same questions.

I've always thought of the Holy Spirit as . . .

_____

_____

When I think of the power God has given me, the first thing that comes to mind is . . .

_____

_____

Circle these True/False statements with your understanding today:

True or False   The Holy Spirit is a person.

True or False   The Holy Spirit speaks directly to Believers in Jesus today.

True or False   The Holy Spirit fills Believers today, supplying supernatural power and wisdom.

True or False   The Holy Spirit gives spiritual gifts to Believers today.

Let's Pray and Press In

I don't know what your relationship with the Holy Spirit has been like in the past. I don't know what you've been taught or who you have known Him to be leading up to this moment. But He wants to meet you as He met me and millions of others. He doesn't want you to be enraptured by just one encounter. He wants to fill you and for you to be aware of His presence continually, every day of your life—each one a reminder of God's purposeful pursuit of your heart.
—*God So Close*

Let's pray and press into the presence of God, who is in the room right now. Let's ask Him to meet with us in this moment. Take a deep breath, and quiet your thoughts.

Father God,

We love You. Thank You for sending Your Holy Spirit for us. We ask now that You'd help us take what we thought we knew about You and clarify it. God, we ask that You'd make us aware of Your presence even now. Help us perceive You in a way we haven't before. We want to meet with You. In Jesus' name we pray. Amen.

Take a minute to listen with your heart. Is the Holy Spirit speaking and revealing the Father's heart to you? Is He revealing God's love for you in a new way? What are you sensing? Close your eyes and

spend some time with the Holy Spirit before writing down what you
are sensing in your spirit.

_____

_____

_____

Remember, the Holy Spirit will be with you wherever you
go. At any moment, you can pause, pray, and press into what He
is saying and doing. Be intentional in the days to come about
taking time to interact with Him.

CHAPTER 2

THE PROMISE OF THE FATHER

Who Is the Holy Spirit?

It was after midnight, and I was in the middle of my freshman year of college. I was stressed by classwork and the drama that comes with roommates and relationships. I can't remember the details of the week except that it was an exceptionally hard one, and I was feeling especially alone.

Worst of all, I couldn't fall asleep that night. I lay there in the dark, praying that God would help me, but I wanted more than a good night of sleep. I needed a Friend. I needed God to come and comfort me. If only He would walk into the room.

I stared into the dark and prayed toward the ceiling, *Jesus, will You come close?*

And then the most surprising and wonderful thing happened.

My attention was drawn to the light that remained on in the hallway of the dormitory at night, and it was as if God Himself was coming toward me. Moments later, peace filled the room.

I knew that I wasn't alone and that the Holy Spirit brought the peace of Jesus to fill my heart. He is our Comforter, and He makes Jesus real to us.

Let's Pause and Ponder

The night God comforted me in my dorm room, it was the Holy Spirit who came to be with me. He revealed the peace of Jesus (who is called the Prince of Peace).

When it comes to the comforting and empowering work of the Holy Spirit, I believe we often attribute to Jesus the work that the Holy Spirit has done within us. Perhaps it's because it is easier for our minds to imagine Jesus coming to us with His kind face and caring arms as our protective but unseen Friend. But an important step in growing our relationship with the Holy Spirit is recognizing that He is our Comforter and Helper.

The Holy Spirit has been sent from the Father to be with us. Can you think of a moment when the Holy Spirit brought you an understanding of the peace or comfort of Jesus? What about supernatural strength to face a hard situation? Or abundant joy in the midst of grief?

_____

_____

Chapter 2 of *God So Close* carefully examines the personhood of the Holy Spirit. He has a mind, will, and emotions. Why do you think it is important to remember the Holy Spirit is a person when interacting with Him?

_____

_____

_____

God So Close Chapter Questions

I think there is confusion in the Church surrounding the Holy Spirit because . . .

_____

_____

_____

When it comes to the personhood of the Holy Spirit, I want to better understand . . .

_____

_____

_____

Let's Pray and Press In

We've reviewed some important themes from chapter 2. Now let's take our process a step further. Let's pray to the Father and press into the presence of the Holy Spirit. Keep this thought close as we pray: the same God who filled Jesus is with you this very moment.

> _Father God,_
>
> _We don't want to overlook Your Holy Spirit ever again. We recognize now He is a person, and He is a gift to our lives. We can know Your Son because the Holy Spirit reveals Him to us. Now we ask that You would increase our perception of His presence and power. Help us remain aware of Your nearness, God. We make space in our lives now for whatever the Holy Spirit wants to do and say to us. Continue to bring us under-standing. In Jesus' name we pray. Amen._

Friend, you have known the Holy Spirit for as long as you have known Jesus. You might not have realized who was comforting or empowering or giving you peace or patience or joy, but Scripture is clear that the Holy Spirit is at work in the lives of those who follow Jesus. Let's press into His presence and ask the Holy Spirit a few questions.

Holy Spirit, we know You're with us. Show us where You have met us in the past. When were You moving in our lives and perhaps we didn't even perceive it to be You? Take a moment and write what comes to mind or what He speaks to your heart.

_____

_____

_____

Holy Spirit, what do You want us to know as we move forward?

_____

_____

_____

As you go through the coming days, remember that the Holy Spirit is a person you can know for yourself. Be sure to take some time in the middle of your ordinary moments to stop and consider that God Himself is with you.

CHAPTER 3

THE BREATH OF GOD

God Is as Close as Your Breath

I was sitting on my back porch looking out at the October Sunday afternoon, thinking about the week ahead. Inside my house, I had a sick middle schooler who was going to miss another week of class. I had a list as long as you can imagine of situations that required my immediate attention. I had worries that wouldn't quiet, thinning patience, and the wave of overwhelm barreling toward the shoreline of my heart. The reality of the week to come was understandably stressful. But as I sat and let the autumn breeze blow over me, I felt the Holy Spirit remind me that this world and what I feel and experience aren't all there is to know.

My friend, we live in the world we can see, which is full of cool October days, busy schedules, and perhaps stressful situations. We are also fully alive in the unseen eternal world, which existed before us and will continue forever. The truth is, both worlds are real, but we often spend much of our time focused on what takes place in the world that will pass away rather than the world that will carry on into eternity. And when we shift our perspectives from what we see around us to what we know is true spiritually, it puts into proper place our attention and expectation for what God can do.

Let's Pause and Ponder

From the moment we were created and God breathed His Spirit into us, He has been as close as our breath. Take a deep breath in, friend . . . He is that close.
—God So Close

Chapter 3 of God So Close asks you where you imagine God to be right now, in this moment. Do you imagine Him in heaven? Or do you think of Him there with you in the room? Take a moment to journal your response. Where do you imagine God in your daily life?

_____

_____

_____

We know God's Spirit fills us, and He doesn't leave us. So the only thing that changes is our perception of His nearness. Have you

ever experienced a time when God seemed especially close or
exceptionally far away? When?

_____

_____

_____

God So Close Chapter Questions

Why would you say it is important to remember that God is always
with us?

_____

_____

_____

In your own words, why do you think a person might overlook the
presence of the Holy Spirit in the room? Do you tend to overlook
the presence of the Holy Spirit in the room with you?

_____

_____

_____

Let's Pray and Press In

We've reviewed some important themes from chapter 3. Now let's take our journey a step further. Let's pray to the Father and press into the presence of the Holy Spirit. Keep this thought close as we pray: God Himself "gives everyone life and breath and everything else" (Acts 17:25).

> *Father God,*
>
> *We are grateful for the eternal life You've given us. Your breath fills us. Your life brings hope to the dead places in our hearts. As we press into Your presence, help us focus on what You are doing. Turn our attention to Your nearness and what Your nearness means for everything we are facing. We ask in Jesus' name. Amen.*

Holy Spirit, what do You want to show us right now about the situations we are facing? Take a moment and write what comes to mind.

_____

_____

_____

_____

_____

**We have an attentive God who is continually
with us, who listens for us as a parent listens
for the cry of his child and responds.**
—*God So Close*

Take a moment to share with God what you want Him to know
about how you feel. Then listen and write down the response of the
Holy Spirit.

_____

_____

_____

**No matter how we feel and no matter the season
or situation, God is constantly close all the time.**
—*God So Close*

God doesn't come and go, but our focus on Him often does.
As you go through the coming days, ask the Holy Spirit to keep
you aware of His involvement in what you see around you.

CHAPTER 4

THE HOLINESS OF GOD

Why the Wrath of God Matters

It was a big deal when my oldest son, Kolton, started morning preschool a few days a week. As a stay-at-home momma, I had been with him nearly every moment for three years, and now he would be making memories and experiencing new events without me.

He always had so much to share when I picked him up from class. One beautiful September day, I barely had the chance to ask, "What was the best part of your day—" when he interrupted, "Mommy! Did you know I'm a sinner?"

"Who told you that you are a sinner?" I asked.

"My teacher!" Kolton answered. "My teacher says we are all sinners!"

He wasn't wrong. We are surely all sinners, but there is important information that should follow that statement. We are sinners who have the opportunity to be saved by grace through faith in Jesus. I'm a firm believer that anytime we are made aware of our sinful selves, we should also be reminded that Jesus made a way for us to be redeemed.

"Did your teachers tell you that Jesus made a way for your sins to be forgiven?" I asked, wondering if there was more to the lesson.

"Nope!"

When I went up to the preschool later that morning to confirm what my son had shared, I was told that they would learn about salvation as part of their Easter lessons in April. For more than six months, these little kiddos would have only half of the story. The presentation of sin wasn't the problem; the presentation of sin without the rest of the gospel message was.

Now, I need to clarify something. Kolton had learned at home about sin, God's love, and God's rescue plan to save us. But I hadn't ever presented sin as a stand-alone concept. Why? Because sin is only part of the picture. Sin and salvation are aspects of one big story.

We should not learn that we are sinners separated from God without also learning that He mercifully made a way for us to be saved. Likewise, we cannot know that from which we have been saved unless we first understand that we are sinners separated from a holy God.

This is what we addressed in chapter 4 of *God So Close*. While much of our understanding of salvation comes from the picture of Jesus' sacrifice, it seems many Christians have missed the concept of God's holiness and wrath that falls on all sinners separated from His presence. We tend to give our full attention to Jesus and His love, but we skip over the fact that our kind, loving, gracious God is also an all-consuming fire.

My friend, without an understanding of God's holiness and the wrath from which we have been spared, how can we fully appreciate the sacrifice of Jesus? And without seeing God as a consuming fire, how are we supposed to feel awe or the reverence of His Holy Spirit, who chooses to dwell within us?

Let's Pause and Ponder

Chapter 4 of God So Close defines the word holy. As you were reading, what came to mind when you thought of the word holiness?

_____

_____

_____

Have you ever wondered how God can be good and loving and still pour out His wrath on His creation? How did the simple illustration of God's wrath in this chapter help your understanding?

_____

_____

_____

In what ways does understanding the holiness of God and seeing God as a consuming fire change your attitude toward the Holy Spirit?

_____

_____

_____

God So Close Chapter Questions

In what ways do you think God's wrath and holiness are connected?

_____

_____

How do you view the love of God and the sacrifice of Jesus in light of what we discussed in this chapter?

_____

_____

Let's Pray and Press In

In my most reverential moments of worship to the Lord, I focus my heart on the reality that God, as an all-consuming fire, still allows me to be in His presence. I'm more than allowed to stand there and simply be near Him; He invites me in to know Him and carry His Holy Spirit within me.

When we have a proper perspective of the holiness of God, it creates a deeper intimacy of our hearts toward Him. He's not just the "Holy" Spirit in title alone. He is the Holy God who calls us closer to His heart. Keep this thought close as we pray: "God has not destined us for wrath, but to obtain salvation through our Lord Jesus Christ" (1 Thessalonians 5:9 ESV).

Father God,

We come before You with awe and reverence. You have made a way for us to be near to You, and often we overlook the profound reality that we are allowed into Your presence as such imperfect people. We couldn't earn this place, but You gave us access to Your heart freely by sending Jesus so that His love and perfection could cover our imperfections. We join the angels in worship right now. We recognize Your holiness! We cry out with them, "Holy, holy, holy is the LORD Almighty; the whole earth is full of his glory" (Isaiah 6:3). Help us keep a proper perspective of who You are so that we never find it ordinary that we are able to draw near to You. In Jesus' name we pray. Amen.

With the foundation of what we have discussed about the Holy Spirit in the last four chapters, let's take just a moment and worship God.

Isaiah 12:1–3 expresses a song of praise. Where it says *anger,* think of *wrath* instead.

> "I will praise you, LORD.
> Although you were angry with me,

your anger has turned away
and you have comforted me.
Surely God is my salvation;
I will trust and not be afraid.
The LORD, the LORD himself, is my strength and
        my defense;
he has become my salvation."
With joy you will draw water
from the wells of salvation.

Take a moment to journal your own prayer and worship.

_____

_____

_____

_____

Holy Spirit, You are more than holy in name. You are holy in nature. We are in awe, and we pause to listen for Your voice. What is the Holy Spirit saying to you? Write what you are sensing Him speak to your heart.

_____

_____

_____

Remember, we are called to be holy as God is holy (1 Peter 1:16). This doesn't mean He expects us to be perfect. It means God wants to help us grasp the meaning of living a life set apart for Him. Spend some time in the days to come meditating on the depths of Jesus' sacrifice and on the fact that a blameless God suffered on our behalf so we wouldn't have to endure His wrath.

CHAPTER 5

THE HOLY FIRE OF GOD

God Manifests His Presence

A sk anyone close to me and they will tell you that I cry easily. I cry at certain movies. I cry during holiday TV commercials. I cry when my children remind me just how much they've grown, and I see how quickly life is passing. I often cry when my husband gives me a sincere compliment. I cry when the underdog in any story overcomes. I would say that I'm a sensitive person, deeply in touch with my own feelings. Crying is not unusual for me. However, there are moments when my tears don't seem natural. They seem to be a physical response to the supernatural world around me.

I remember standing in a worship service shortly after we had moved to California from our home in Oklahoma. I missed my family, and it would have made sense for the emotion of the morning to come through and for tears to fall as I thought about how far away they felt. But as I began to sing, my attention shifted from my family's distance to God's presence.

It was as if He was standing next to me, telling me that He had a plan, and it was good. I heard Him reassure me that we could trust Him, and He was in fact leading us. It was in this moment that I began to cry not because I was sad but because I felt loved. God had manifested His love for me in a way that moved beyond what my mind understood and translated into what my heart could feel and perceive.

We might not think of moments like these as an encounter with the Spirit of God manifesting His love to us. We might think we were simply moved emotionally. But I wonder how often we have attributed to our emotions what the Holy Spirit was actually doing within us. It's not that God is changing His position of proximity to us. It's simply that He is revealing His nearness and our physical bodies are responding to the revelation of God in the room.

Let's Pause and Ponder

Have you ever stood in worship and been moved to tears by God's love? That was the Holy Spirit manifesting God's love for you. Have you ever felt anxious and prayed and then suddenly felt calm? That was the Holy Spirit manifesting God's peace to you. What about joy? I can think of a time when my heart felt burdened, and as I prayed and turned my attention from the problem to His presence, I felt joy replacing the stress.

Write out one moment when you didn't just know God was close, but you felt Him moving in your heart.

_____

_____

_____

> **Wouldn't you imagine that if Jesus walked into the room, your heart might skip a beat or you might be moved to tears? Why then should it be any different for the same Spirit who filled Him to move in our hearts and draw a reaction from us?**
> —*God So Close*

How would you respond if Jesus walked into the room right now? How does your answer to that question compare with how you tend to respond to the presence of the Holy Spirit in your daily life?

_____

_____

_____

What do you want to learn in regard to the manifestation of God's presence?

_____

_____

Chapter 5 of *God So Close* takes a close look at the manifest presence of God as He came down on the mountain in fire in Exodus 19:16–19. Sometimes our minds have a hard time fully comprehending that this same God is the one who comes close to us now. This is the same God who manifests His presence to us today. As you read the words about the Israelites' encounter with Him, how does it change your perspective of the Holy Spirit's nearness to us now?

_____

_____

In the previous chapter, we talked about how a holy God could not come near an unholy people. Remember the example of God's bubble of perfection I gave to my children? Chapter 5 of the book explains that God gave the Israelites a set of rules called the Law. The Law, and the Israelites' obedience to follow it, made a way for God to come near His people until Jesus came to be the ultimate sacrifice. How does God giving His children the Law demonstrate His desire to be with them?

_____

_____

God So Close Chapter Questions

Have you ever experienced a time when God moved near you or through you? What happened?

_____

_____

How do you view the fire of God after reading this chapter?

_____

_____

Let's Pray and Press In

As we pray together, let's keep this thought at the front of our minds:

**The fire of God has not burned out. He has
not changed and cannot change. . . . He
is right there, moving in your midst.**
—God So Close

Father God,

_We know that You have been near, but we want to recognize
Your presence moving with us. Like the Israelites, we want to see_

You and hear You and be in awe of Your power yet humbled by Your love. Teach us, like children, what we have already sensed in our spirits. Give us an understanding of what we've previously perceived so we don't miss one moment in the future of understanding that You are near. Use us to accomplish Your purposes. Use us to reach others with the powerful, personal, and perfect love You offer us. In Jesus' name we pray. Amen.

Let's ask the Holy Spirit to reveal His presence to us right now. Let's press into what we are sensing as we pray, as Moses did, "Now show [us] your glory" (Exodus 33:18).

Holy Spirit, we know You are with us. We pause and simply ask You to help us perceive Your nearness. Take a moment to write what He is saying and what you are sensing.

_____

_____

_____

_____

Is there anything you want God to know about how you feel? Of course, He already knows every detail, but just as a parent wants to hear from his child even if he knows the facts, God wants us to share our hearts with Him.

What do you want God to know right now about how you feel or what you're going through?

_____

_____

_____

Before you move on to the next chapter, take a moment to reflect on this: everything God has given you was to draw you back into a relationship with Him—not so you could simply say you know Him but so you could experience a life awakened to His presence with you. In the coming days, pay careful attention to when you need God's help and how He manifests Himself when you call.

CHAPTER 6

THE OUTPOURING OF THE HOLY SPIRIT

What Pentecost Means for You

Some of my favorite stories in Scripture take place on the water. There's a story about Jesus walking on top of the water to reach His disciples in a boat after they had already set out onto the lake earlier in the day (Matthew 14:22–33). There's another story about Jesus sleeping in a boat during a storm (Mark 4:35–41). We can't forget the story of Noah and his ark (Genesis 6–9), or the story of Jesus helping Peter miraculously catch fish from the side of his boat (Luke 5:1–11). Water and boats are commonly used to illustrate lessons throughout the Bible, and I've heard countless messages at churches comparing our lives as Christians to these familiar stories.

But have you ever heard that the most accurate depiction of

a Christian's life isn't a boat that successfully navigates troubled seas? The best illustration of our lives as followers of Jesus is actually a sunken ship. Here's what I mean.

If you're familiar with the Bible, you likely know about John the Baptist. He did important work, pointing his followers to Jesus, who was coming soon. He said publicly, "I baptize with water. . . . But someone is coming soon who is greater than I am. . . . He [Jesus] will baptize you with the Holy Spirit and with fire" (Matthew 3:11 NLT). According to *Strong's Concordance*, the word used here for "baptize" is *baptizó*. It means "to dip," but it also means "to sink." An accurate picture of this word is a sunken vessel with water not only around it but also within it.

Let's imagine that for just a moment. When Jesus became the Lord of our lives, Scripture says that God gave us His Spirit: "This is how we know that we live in him and he in us: He has given us of his Spirit" (1 John 4:13). The Spirit of God isn't just around us like water surrounding a boat, carried along by its waves. We are submerged in His presence. We have been baptized with the Holy Spirit, who now fills us. John the Baptist dipped people into the water, but Jesus placed the fire of the Holy Spirit within us. What a picture! What a reality!

The Holy Spirit of God fills you as He filled Jesus.

Let's Pause and Ponder

You have the Holy Spirit inside of you as a believer of Jesus. However, chapter 6 of *God So Close* invites you to answer this question:

**Did you know that if you want to experience
a greater measure of God's Spirit filling
you, all you have to do is ask?**
—God So Close

There's a story found in Acts 8 about a town in Samaria receiving the Holy Spirit:

> When the apostles in Jerusalem heard that Samaria had accepted the word of God, they sent Peter and John to Samaria. When they arrived, they prayed for the new believers there that they might receive the Holy Spirit, because the Holy Spirit had not yet come on any of them; they had simply been baptized in the name of the Lord Jesus. Then Peter and John placed their hands on them, and they received the Holy Spirit. (vv. 14–17)

In another account, Peter shared the message of Jesus with a family, and while he was speaking, the Holy Spirit came on all who heard the message (Acts 10:23–44). There is another recorded instance when Paul found Believers in Jesus and asked if they had received the Holy Spirit when they believed. They said they hadn't even heard there was a Holy Spirit. Paul baptized them in the name of Jesus and then placed his hands on them and prayed, and they received the Holy Spirit (Acts 19:1–6).

I highlight these stories because I want you to notice something. While the details are slightly different, there was a powerful encounter between the Believers and the Holy Spirit in each of them. Men and women received the Holy Spirit, and each time it was evident that He had filled them in a unique way.

I love A. W. Tozer's quote included in the book: "I do not find in the Old Testament or in the New Testament, neither in Christian biography, in church history or in personal Christian testimonies, the experience of any person who was ever filled with the Holy Spirit and didn't know it!"

So ponder this with me for just a moment before we move on to pray and press in.

What does Scripture say about the Holy Spirit filling Believers? Take some time to read Acts 2, 8, 10, and 19 and write what stands out to you.

_____

_____

_____

_____

God So Close Chapter Questions

After reading this chapter, how would you explain what it means to be "filled with the Spirit"?

_____

_____

Have you ever had an experience of being filled with the Spirit? If so, what happened? If not, ask God to fill you afresh with His Spirit.

_____

_____

_____

_____

Let's Pray and Press In

> We can ask and continue to ask for a fresh outpouring of God's Spirit into our hearts. . . . He is the all-consuming, fire-sending, earth-quaking, life-changing, dead-awakening Spirit of the Holy God, and He wants to fill you with His power so that you can know Him for yourself and carry the truth of Jesus into the world around you.
> —God So Close

The Holy Spirit is right here with us. Let's ask Him to fill us with His power and love. Pray this or speak to the Father using your own words:

Father God,
I ask that You would pour out Your Spirit into my heart in

a fresh way. I know the Holy Spirit is constantly present, but I want to be filled to overflowing. I want to ask and continue to ask to receive the Holy Spirit as the gift You've intended Him to be in my life. Like rushing wind, come and blow through my heart in a fresh way. I want to know You fully, I want to hear You clearly, and I want Your Spirit to overflow from within me. Thank You for this promise of Your presence. In Jesus' name I pray. Amen.

Take a moment to write what the Holy Spirit is saying and what you are sensing.

_____

_____

_____

_____

I encourage you to take a few moments to think about the holy fire of God that descended onto the mountain and now fills your heart. Are there words of praise or worship you want to say to God? Spend a few moments in worship, and write down what comes to your heart as you think of His holiness and His presence.

_____

_____

_____

_____

The *same* Holy Spirit who filled Jesus, Peter, John, Paul, and countless others also fills *you*. Spend some time focused on this truth in the days to come.

CHAPTER 7

THE GOD WHO SPEAKS

God Has Not Lost His Voice

Beginning in kindergarten, the only thing I really ever got in real trouble for during school was my inability to stop talking to my classmates. Now, don't get me wrong. I knew I wasn't supposed to talk when the teacher was talking, when we were supposed to be focused on working, or when a book was being read to us as we gathered on the floor to listen. (Poor Courtney Johnston. I took her down with me as we were both moved to opposite ends of the reading rug.) I understood all these things. But there were times when my mouth would open, and words would just spill out as if I had to say them or I'd explode.

The truth is, for my entire life, the thoughts in my head have found their way out of my mouth even when I'm supposed to be silent. Silence just doesn't come naturally for me. Considering the hundreds of thousands of words I've penned into books, now I'm grateful that God gave me a love of words and made me chatty like Him.

That's how I think of God—as chatty. We're both talkers. Have you ever stopped to think about how much God's voice plays a part in who He is? Jesus is called the *Word*. "The *Word* became flesh and made his dwelling among us" (John 1:14). God *spoke* the world into existence, *saying*, "Let there be light" (Genesis 1:3). The Bible is filled with God's spoken words to His people and the recorded words of Jesus. And the entire Bible is evidence of His desire to communicate with us.

As chapter 7 of *God So Close* states, "I often wonder why some would believe He has said all there is to say." God has not lost His voice, and He continues to speak to us today.

Let's Pause and Ponder

The Father sent the Son so our relationship with Him could be restored, and one of the benefits of this restored relationship is our ability to hear from the Holy Spirit as He continually speaks from within us.
—God So Close

Can you think of a time when you clearly heard the voice of the Lord? What did He say?

_____

_____

_____

_____

Jesus said, "I have much more to say to you, more than you can now bear. But when he, the Spirit of truth, comes, he will guide you into all the truth. He will not speak on his own; he will speak only what he hears, and he will tell you what is yet to come" (John 16:12–13).

Since Jesus made it clear that the Holy Spirit would speak what He hears the Father say, how does hearing the voice of the Holy Spirit help you better know the Father?

_____

_____

_____

_____

In what ways would you listen for the Holy Spirit throughout your day if you remembered He wants to speak to you?

_____

_____

_____

God So Close Chapter Questions

Why is it important to remember that God has not lost His voice?

_____

_____

_____

How would it affect your relationship with God to believe He speaks directly to your heart today?

_____

_____

_____

Let's Pray and Press In

As we pray together, let's focus on this important truth:

> **The voice that created all things, holds together**
> **all things, and through whom all things were made**
> **(Colossians 1:16–17) still whispers within us.**
> —*God So Close*

Father God,

We thank You that You made us to hear Your voice. We were created with the ability to respond when You speak. And now You speak and lead and love from within us. Help us remember that You haven't lost Your voice—that it's not possible for You to lose Your voice. You can't change, and You're a speaking God. Your Spirit testifies within us of what Jesus has done. Keep our ears tuned to what You are saying. In Jesus' name we pray. Amen.

Holy Spirit, what do You want to reveal to us? What are You saying right now? We are listening. Take a moment to write what you sense the Holy Spirit is speaking to your heart.

_____

_____

_____

Is there something you want to tell God? Take a minute to continue your conversation with Him. Write your response to what He is saying.

_____

_____

_____

Remember, the same voice that spoke from the billowing clouds that covered the mountain of God now speaks from within your own heart. The same power, but so much closer. Isn't He wonderful?

CHAPTER 8

THE VOICE OF THE LORD

God Wants Us to Hear Him

When I was growing up, there was an elderly woman who attended our downtown Oklahoma City church. She would occasionally hear a clear message from the Lord and share it with the congregation during the service. Looking back, I'm so grateful for the way our pastor made a space for her to do that, and he always explained what was going on to those who might not understand.

Her words seemed to carry a holy weight to them. They were directional and powerful. It seemed as if God was speaking right to us, using this kind woman's voice as His microphone. I couldn't help but wonder, however, why God didn't speak to all of us. I was grateful to have heard from Him through her words, but I wondered why He seemed to have chosen only her.

That church was formative in much of what I learned about

God. However, I didn't gain a full understanding of the different ways God speaks while there. I knew He spoke through the Bible and pastors and kind old women who delivered a message like a letter from heaven during a worship service, but I hadn't yet learned that God speaks to all Christians. And I definitely didn't know that God speaks to His children in so many different ways.

It wasn't until I was enrolled in Bible college that the Holy Spirit began leading me to books and sermons that explained in great detail the ways our spirits perceive God's voice. That is when I learned that all Believers do hear from God. Perhaps we just haven't recognized what we were perceiving as His voice.

As Believers who are filled with the Holy Spirit and awakened to His presence, we must remember this:

> **His voice continues to speak to us, using multiple methods that we often perceive through our spiritual senses. We just need to learn to tune those senses to His presence.**
> —God So Close

Let's Pause and Ponder

I think the way I felt as a young child is common. After all, when someone professes to hear God speak so clearly, while we cannot point to a moment when we have been confident that He spoke to us, it makes us wonder, *Does He even speak to me?*

As you have been reading, have you thought, *Why does God seem to speak so clearly to others? How can I recognize His voice in my daily life?* Do you think this is the way many Believers feel?

_____

_____

_____

Throughout chapter 8 of *God So Close*, we looked at the various ways our spirits perceive the voice of the Holy Spirit. Can you think of people in your life who seem to hear from God in an unusual way? Who are they, and what have they shared with you?

_____

_____

_____

God So Close Chapter Questions

What is one moment when you heard God speak clearly in the past?

_____

_____

In what way(s) do you hear from God most often?

_____

_____

_____

Let's Pray and Press In

Focus on this thought with me for just a moment: God designed you to hear His voice and began calling your heart to His long ago. Your spirit recognizes Him even if your mind doesn't understand what you sense as Him. As we pray, remember that God wants to speak to you even more than you want to hear Him.

Father God,

We do believe You have spoken to us. We do trust that You have been the one to lead us all along. We ask that You would bring to our remembrance all the moments we have heard from You in the past. Help us use those times to train our spiritual sense to perceive when You are speaking today. You're a creative God who sent Your Holy Spirit to be with us. He speaks what He hears. So help us hear what He speaks. In Jesus' name we pray. Amen.

Press into what you are perceiving from the Holy Spirit. How is He speaking to you? What are you sensing? Is He showing you something? Is He whispering something? Do you sense Him wanting to remind you of something right now? Like Samuel, we say, "Speak, LORD, for your servant is listening" (1 Samuel 3:9). Describe what you perceive to be hearing from God.

_____

_____

_____

Is there something you want to tell God? Take a minute to continue your conversation with Him. Write your response to what He is saying or what You perceive He is telling you.

_____

_____

_____

Now that you have journaled what God is showing you, is there anything you want to ask Him? Take a moment to journal your personal prayer below.

_____

_____

_____

When we believe that God still speaks and we are capable of hearing Him, everything about ordinary life changes. Keep your heart tuned to His voice in the days ahead. He has something important to tell you.

CHAPTER 9

THE PROMPTING OF THE SPIRIT

How to Be Sure It's His Voice

When I was little, I loved watching the TV show *The Price Is Right*. It aired while I was at school, but this show was one sunny spot on days when I'd be home sick or out of class for a dentist appointment. Are you familiar with this program?

Selected audience members are invited out of the crowd to *Come on down!* to the front, where they compete with a handful of other guests to guess the price of a retail item. The contestant who makes the closest guess without going over the actual retail price of the item is invited up to the stage, where they participate in various other games of guessing prices.

Hence the name, *The Price Is Right*.

A hallmark of this show is that audience participation is

welcomed as the contestant attempts to make their guesses. The contestant on stage looks to the shouting crowd and listens as the roar of suggestions echoes back toward them. The camera, often staying focused on the contestant, captures their eyes peering into the audience and their physical gestures as they do their best to communicate with friends or relatives offering their help on the other side of the set.

Truthfully, it was always a dream of mine to be on the show, and often I wondered what that would be like to bring my family and try to listen for their voices over the hundreds of others telling me what they thought was best. Would it even be possible?

Here's what I think. When you have spent so much time with someone, I believe it is *very* possible to hear a familiar voice even in a crowd of others. Just ask my seven-year-old son, who currently dislikes when I offer soccer "suggestions" loudly from the sidelines. It doesn't matter how many other mommas and daddies are offering support to their players, my son recognizes the sound of my voice (and often responds by holding his finger up to his lips to say, "Shh"). He might not enjoy hearing me, but the point of the matter remains the same. When we know someone well, we can easily recognize when they are speaking and what they are directing us to do even when there is plenty of noise competing for our attention.

Let's Pause and Ponder

Chapter 9 of *God So Close* outlines questions we can ask ourselves when we believe God is speaking to us or directing us in some way.

Does the Bible confirm what I'm hearing?
Does what I'm hearing sound like Jesus?
Does what I'm hearing lead toward God or away from Him?
Does this message testify of the work of Jesus?

Notice that three out of four of these questions involve knowing Scripture and the recorded words and works of Jesus. In your own words, explain how discerning God's voice is closely linked to what we know of Him through the evidence of Scripture.

_____

_____

_____

Sometimes we want wisdom or direction without the time it takes to listen for God's voice. We want Him to drop information into our lives like a text on our phone, an email in the inbox, or even a letter in the mail. The reality is, He wants our attention. He wants a relationship with us. We can have conversations with Him, which means we must learn how to listen.

How often do you make time to listen for God's voice so that you might become more familiar with His daily promptings?

_____

_____

There have been plenty of times in my life when I've wondered, *Is this really God leading me? How can I be sure it's what He wants me to do?* Have you ever experienced the same? If so, describe the situation.

_____

_____

_____

God So Close Chapter Questions

Has God ever asked you to do something that seemed out of the ordinary? If so, how did you know it was Him?

_____

_____

_____

In what ways do you think recognizing God's voice changes over the course of time you spend speaking with Him?

_____

_____

_____

Let's Pray and Press In

As we pray, remember that God isn't just involved in speaking to our hearts. He is also helping us listen and discern His voice.

> **There is no supernatural process—including speaking to and hearing from God—that we carry out in our own strength. Rather, it is the work of the Holy Spirit, at work within us, who teaches us to discern the voice of the Lord.**
> —God So Close

Father God, we stop in the middle of everything else going on to just listen for Your voice.

Our journey through this book has been one where we have shared our hearts with You. We have asked for wisdom to learn when You are speaking to us. Now, without any other agenda other than to simply hear from You and become familiar with Your voice, we ask that You'd speak to us. We are listening, God. What do You want to say?

Thank You, Lord, for Your nearness. Thank You for the closeness available through the Holy Spirit. Awaken us to Your presence and the power of Your voice. In Jesus' name we pray. Amen.

In the days ahead, create a physical space in your day to listen for what God is saying. Spend moments reading His Word so you can become familiar with the way He speaks and who He is. And finally, remember this:

He is a God who can be known,
and He remains so close.
—*God So Close*

CHAPTER 10

THE DIRECTION
OF THE SPIRIT

The Holy Spirit Leads You Today

Everyone was busy. My husband was at work, my kids were at school, my parents and my in-laws were at appointments, my friends were dealing with their own life issues—and I needed advice. I needed to know what to do next. I just needed some clear direction.

I remember walking through my house thinking, *There's no one left to call. How do I make the right choice when there's no one to ask for counsel?* I looked out the bedroom window at the trees, and I felt the Holy Spirit remind me of an important truth—the same truth I shared throughout chapter 10 of *God So Close*. The Holy Spirit wants to lead me. He has all the wisdom I need to make the right decision. And all I have to do is ask.

I'd share the full details of the story—what exactly I was trying to decide and all of the drama surrounding my options—but they don't really matter. I'm not trying to tell you how I had a grand revelation and eventually came up with the perfect choice. The point I'm trying to make is that even when we know the Holy Spirit wants to lead us, we often exhaust all our physical options before we consult Him for His godly direction. The truth is, God wants us to remember in all situations, big and small, that He desires to guide us as a faithful God.

A life awakened by the Holy Spirit
is a life that is led by Him.
—God So Close

Let's Pause and Ponder

What if you were to wake up tomorrow morning and breathe in and out, welcoming the presence of God in your lungs, and ask God to fill you with His wisdom so you knew which choices to make throughout the day? How would the places you go, the conversations you have, and the thoughts you think change if you could keep in the front of your mind the truth that the Spirit desires to lead you? How would you live differently if you had more awareness that He is present and ready to guide you into a deeper understanding of who God is so that you can serve and trust Him wholeheartedly? Take some time to ponder these questions and journal your responses below.

_____

_____

All that we are reading, learning, and discussing in this guidebook is so that we can experience a deeper, more loving relationship with God. Why do you think it is important to remember that you are led by a God who loves you?

_____

_____

Take a moment to read through Paul and Silas's experience in jail and the events that followed in Acts 16:25–40. Why is it important to remember that a Spirit-led life isn't free from trial?

_____

_____

God So Close Chapter Questions

Can you think of a time when you sensed peace in making a decision? What happened?

_____

_____

Have you experienced a time when God led you in a direction that didn't make sense? If so, what was the outcome of following Him?

_____

_____

_____

_____

Let's Pray and Press In

Proverbs 3:5–6 says, "Trust in the LORD with all your heart and lean not on your own understanding; in all your ways submit to him, and he will make your paths straight."

Let's take a moment to thank God for being the one who directs our paths and makes them straight. And then let's ask Him to give us wisdom and direction for the steps ahead.

Father God,

Thank You for being faithful. We can place our full trust in You because You have proven again and again that You will not let us down. You will lead us with peace. Your love will be evident in every step You ask us to take. We are so grateful for how You have led us in the past. And now we ask You to show us what to do next, trusting that You will continue to be faithful to lead us in love. In Jesus' name we pray. Amen.

Take a moment to write out where you need direction right now, trusting that God desires to lead you toward tomorrow with "hope and a future" (Jeremiah 29:11).

_____

_____

_____

> [The Holy Spirit] walked with Jesus all the way to
> the cross, and He remains with us always—through
> every victory and every valley. He won't ever
> lead us to a place where He will not go as well.
> —*God So Close*

As you look toward the coming days, remember exactly who you are trusting with your next steps. Deuteronomy 7:9 says this of Him: "Know therefore that the LORD your God is God; he is the faithful God, keeping his covenant of love to a thousand generations of those who love him and keep his commandments." He is the faithful God. Amen.

CHAPTER 11

THE PROPHETIC WORD

How to Hear God for Others

It was shortly after my first encounter with the Holy Spirit described in chapter 1 of *God So Close* that I received the first prophetic word of my life from someone who didn't know me at all. We were in another worship service on the East Coast. We had been invited to hear a guest speaker from another country who had a radical testimony of miraculous healing.

It was in that service that I saw God perform miracles that you might not believe if I were to write them here. Yet, because of what I saw, I can never be convinced that God doesn't still perform miracles. I saw them with my own eyes. It was a life-shaping event for me. But it wasn't just because of what I saw. It was also at this service that God used a person to speak a specific message to me for the first time.

At the end of the service, there was a time of prayer. People ran to the altar to be prayed for, and I was one of them. The familiar sweetness and peace of the Holy Spirit settled over the room, and my eyes were closed as I listened to the people around me and their worshipful words and the powerful prayers spoken.

It wasn't a quiet event. Many people were praying out loud for others. Many people were singing, and some were crying. But it wasn't unsettling. It was actually full of hope and joy and the presence of the Holy Spirit.

A kind old woman lovingly called Sister Naomi was praying for my family one by one. She wasn't just speaking her own thoughts. She asked God to bless us and use us; and as she spoke, she listened for the voice of the Holy Spirit and said what she heard Him speaking. It was powerful.

When she came to me, I heard her say, "The Lord says, 'You will preach and teach at a young age. You will walk in the miraculous and be carried by My Spirit.'" I heard those words with my ears, but I also felt them in my spirit. They weren't just air and sound; they were full of the Spirit and life (John 6:63).

From that moment, my life was marked in a unique way. I knew God was asking me to spread the gospel and revive hearts with the power of the Holy Spirit. I believed what God had said about me through this woman. I suppose you could say that, twenty-five years later, this guidebook in your hands is the evidence of her faithfully hearing and speaking that prophetic word from the Holy Spirit.

Not all prophetic words are like hers. As we discussed in chapter 11 of God So Close, a prophetic word is God speaking through us to strengthen, encourage, and comfort. And that is something we can all do and should eagerly desire.

Simply put, we have the ability to listen to the Holy Spirit and prophesy the good news of Jesus.
—God So Close

Let's Pause and Ponder

Has anyone ever shared something with you that you can see now was God speaking to your heart through that person?

_____

_____

_____

The steps that we use when discerning the voice of the Lord for ourselves are the same questions we ask when listening to what we sense God saying for others:

- *Does the Bible confirm what I am hearing?*
- *Does what I'm hearing sound like Jesus?*
- *Does what I'm hearing lead this person toward God or away from Him?*
- *Does this message testify of the work of Jesus?*

How do you suppose listening for the Holy Spirit and then discerning His voice for the world around us could be a tool used to share the gospel?

_____

_____

_____

Have you ever felt compassion for someone and wanted to share an encouraging word with her? Have you ever felt hope for someone who seemed discouraged and wanted to remind her what the Bible said about the situation she faced? What happened?

_____

_____

_____

God So Close Chapter Questions

Can you think of a time when you shared something with a friend or loved one that you can see now was likely the prompting of the Holy Spirit? What happened?

_____

_____

72

In your own words, why do you suppose prophecy is something we should eagerly desire?

_____

_____

_____

Let's Pray and Press In

My friend, it is a weighty responsibility to hear from God for others. But it is a beautiful opportunity given to us by the Holy Spirit that requires us to lean into our relationship with Him, and it reminds us just how close He really is.
—God So Close

Keep this in mind as we pray: "The one who prophesies speaks to people for their strengthening, encouraging and comfort" (1 Corinthians 14:3).

Father God,

We lean in and listen for Your voice now speaking louder and clearer than all other competing sounds we hear around and even within our own hearts. Thank You for speaking not just to us but through us. In Jesus' name we pray. Amen.

> **He is always reminding us of what God has
> already accomplished through Jesus. He is
> always speaking of the Father's love for us. He
> is always guiding us toward Him and away from
> sin. And when we interact with others around us,
> we have the ability to hear the truth that God
> has to say about them and say it out loud.**
> —God So Close

What do you suppose God wants to tell your family? Take a
moment to listen to the Holy Spirit, and write what you sense Him
saying about your loved ones.

_____

_____

_____

What do you suppose God wants to say to your friends, neighbors,
or coworkers? Is there anyone in particular the Holy Spirit is
bringing to your mind? Are you seeing a picture in your mind?
Are you sensing hope or love or an encouraging thought? Take a
moment to write what you hear Him speaking to your heart.

_____

_____

**No longer does God only select specific men
[or women] to hear His voice intimately....
[The Holy Spirit] is the one who declares
the mysteries of God directly to us.**
—*God So Close*

Let's listen to Him for the world around us.

CHAPTER 12

THE KNOWLEDGE OF GOD

Things Only God Could Know

Scripture doesn't say how many people were gathered in Capernaum that day, but Mark 2 is clear that as Jesus spoke, there were "such large numbers that there was no room left, not even outside the door" (v. 2). News had traveled that He was a healer, and people were desperate to hear Him and come close to Him. Let's take a look at what happened:

> Some men came, bringing to him a paralyzed man, carried by four of them. Since they could not get him to Jesus because of the crowd, they made an opening in the roof above Jesus by digging through it and then lowered the mat the man was lying on. (vv. 3–4)

Now, this story is surely about this man's healing and the faith of his friends. However, there's something I want to highlight about Jesus in this event. Look at what happened next:

When Jesus saw their faith, he said to the paralyzed man, "Son, your sins are forgiven."

Now some teachers of the law were sitting there, thinking to themselves, "Why does this fellow talk like that? He's blaspheming! Who can forgive sins but God alone?" (vv. 5–7)

Notice that the teachers of the law weren't speaking these words. They were simply "thinking to themselves." But catch what Scripture records about Jesus next:

Immediately *Jesus knew in his spirit* that this was what they were thinking in their hearts, and he said to them, "Why are you thinking these things?" (v. 8)

The verse says that *Jesus knew in His spirit* what they were thinking in their hearts. There is nothing hidden from Him. He knows everything we've done and everything we will ever do.

> **There is nothing unknown to the Spirit of God, and He dwells within us.**
> —God So Close

Let's Pause and Ponder

Prior to reading this chapter, had you ever considered that the Holy Spirit could reveal information to our hearts that we couldn't know any other way? What has your understanding of this topic been in the past?

_____

_____

_____

**I believe we often put limits on the supernatural work
we believe God can accomplish in and through us.**
—*God So Close*

I don't think we put limits on God intentionally. We simply stay focused on what we see and know in the world around us rather than what the Holy Spirit sees and makes known to our spirits within us.

What would happen if we really did choose to pause, listen with our spiritual ears, and look with our spiritual eyes? What would we hear? What would we know? What would God invite us to do together?

Take a moment to write out how it could impact your life to share God's love for others by sharing what the Holy Spirit makes known to your spirit.

_____

_____

_____

There's a story in Scripture about the moment a man named Nathanael met Jesus. They had never met, but as Nathanael walked toward Him, Jesus declared:

"Here truly is an Israelite in whom there is no deceit."

"How do you know me?" Nathanael asked.

Jesus answered, "I saw you while you were still under the fig tree before Philip called you."

Then Nathanael declared, "Rabbi, you are the Son of God; you are the king of Israel."

Jesus said, "You believe because I told you I saw you under the fig tree. You will see greater things than that." (John 1:47–50)

Notice how deeply it impacted Nathanael to hear that Jesus knew the details of his life without ever meeting him in person. Nathanael began to follow Jesus that day, and everything about his life changed.

Did you know that the Holy Spirit can reveal information to our hearts that we couldn't know otherwise? Why would this be a useful tool in sharing the gospel?

_____

_____

_____

_____

God So Close Chapter Questions

Have you ever had a moment when you believed God was telling you something only He could know? What happened?

_____

_____

In your own words, how might it encourage a person to realize that God knows the details of her life and has a plan for her?

_____

_____

Let's Pray and Press In

First Corinthians 2:16 says, "We have the mind of Christ." Let's focus on this truth as we pray together.

Father God,

Your Word teaches us that nothing is impossible for you. Nothing is hidden from You. Nothing is unknown. Just as Jesus in His spirit knew information about others and used it to draw people closer to You, we see the purpose in the Holy Spirit revealing information we couldn't know any other way. Lord, help us use every opportunity to speak hope, healing, or encouragement into someone else's life. This idea might seem hard to comprehend, *but we know that You are helping our minds understand this spiritual truth even now. Just as Paul said to the church in Corinth, "The person without the Spirit does not accept the things that come from the Spirit of God but considers them foolishness, and cannot understand them because they are discerned only through the Spirit" (1 Corinthians 2:14). We know that we have the mind of Christ (1 Corinthians 2:16), and that means this spiritual concept isn't too big or too hard to understand. Continue to teach us and lead us. In Jesus' name we pray. Amen.*

Take a moment to ask the Holy Spirit to explain more about this concept to you. What is He helping you discern?

_____

_____

_____

_____

_____

We don't always know why the Holy Spirit asks us to step out in faith and share His love, but every word of knowledge from the Spirit is like a seed from heaven. We simply have to listen to His voice and trust the power of truth to grow into eternal life once seeded into someone else's heart.

—*God So Close*

Pay careful attention to what the Holy Spirit is revealing to your heart that only He could know. It just might change someone's life.

CHAPTER 13

THE GIFTS OF THE SPIRIT

Why the Body of Christ Needs Your Spiritual Gifts

When you were young, were you ever asked which superpower you'd want if you could choose only one? I have asked my own children this question a number of times as they have grown. Sometimes they say they wish they could fly, or at other times they say they wish they could have super strength. What about you? What superpower would you want? It's fun to think about it, right? The truth is, when the conversation is over, we often shrug and think, *Well, superpowers aren't real anyway. We're just regular people in regular bodies.*

But do you know what? I think that might be one of the Enemy's favorite lies. We might not be able to fly or jump buildings or lift cars, but as Christians who are filled with the Holy

Spirit of God, we actually do possess supernatural gifts and power, as we discussed in chapter 13 of *God So Close*.

In 1 Corinthians 12, we learn that the Holy Spirit gives some people supernatural wisdom, others healing, and others the power to perform miracles. These aren't just ideas. They aren't just a list of previous giftings that had an expiration date. They are real spiritual gifts still available to Christians today, and they require the supernatural presence and power of the Holy Spirit moving through us. The problem is, not all Believers know they are in possession of these gifts. So let's discuss them.

Let's Pause and Ponder

Open your Bible to 1 Corinthians 12:8-10, 28-30 (or use your favorite online search engine to pull up the verses). Take a look at the gifts Paul mentioned, and list them below.

_____

_____

Read Romans 12:6-8 and write the gifts Paul listed.

_____

_____

_____

Paul didn't write to convince the churches that Christians possess these spiritual gifts. He wrote to explain their use. How does this help us understand that it is important for us to know their proper use as well?

_____

_____

_____

We can do nothing for God apart from God (John 15:5). In what ways does using our spiritual gifts grow our relationship with the Holy Spirit?

_____

_____

_____

The spiritual gifts are not just for our own enjoyment. They aren't presents for us to boast in. They are meant to impact the people Jesus wants to touch and speak to; He simply invites our hands, hearts, minds, and voices to be part of His process. As a result, those on the other side of our obedience are touched by the Holy Spirit. The blessing we receive from

using these gifts is the relationship we have with the
Holy Spirit as we allow Him to move through us.
—*God So Close*

God So Close Chapter Questions

Look at the list of spiritual gifts you wrote out previously, or open
your Bible to Romans 12:6–8 and 1 Corinthians 12:8–10, 28–30 and
look at the gifts Paul mentioned. Which ones do you see evident in
your own life?

_____

_____

In your own words, why does the body of Christ need you to
remember you are a Spirit-filled Believer?

_____

_____

Let's Pray and Press In

Let's keep this in mind as we pray: "There are different kinds of
spiritual gifts, but the same Spirit is the source of them all. . . .

A spiritual gift is given to each of us so we can help each other"
(1 Corinthians 12:4, 7 NLT).

> *Father God,*
>
> *We acknowledge now that You have given us gifts so we can better know You, so we share Your love, and so we can be Your hands and feet on the earth. We know that we can do nothing for You apart from You, so through using the gifts You've given us, we see that we can better know You. We pause to ask now, "What can we do together, God?" We yield to Your Spirit and say, "Use us!" In Jesus' name we pray. Amen.*

Holy Spirit, were there moments when You moved through us in the past and we didn't recognize at that time the gift You had given us? Remind us of the moments when Your gifts were evident in our lives. Take a moment and describe what you sense the Holy Spirit reminding you.

_____

_____

Take a moment and speak with God yourself. Tell Him sincerely, *Here I am, Lord. Send me; use me; flow through me!* Ask Him to show you which gifts you have been given or to teach you more about the gifts you have. Write out your own prayer below.

_____

_____

_____

_____

Believe me when I tell you the world needs your spiritual gifts. People in your life need you to show up carrying the power of the Holy Spirit, who is inside of you, and to allow Him to work through you in supernatural ways.

In the days ahead, ask the Holy Spirit to give you opportunities to use your giftings for God's glory.

CHAPTER 14

THE PURSUIT OF GOD

What Do You Seek?

I had never lived in a place where people introduced themselves by their list of accomplishments until Jared and I moved to Los Angeles with our kids in 2017. It was a stark difference from Oklahoma, where people often mentioned their family members and hometown when meeting someone for the first time. In Oklahoma, much of our identity was in who we are related to, while in Los Angeles, the culture seemed more impressed by who you knew and what you had done.

Now, this obviously wasn't true of everyone in either location. Not everyone in Los Angeles gave us a list of movies or projects they had worked on, and not everyone in Oklahoma told us who their parents were when making acquaintances. But, in our experience, these two observations were true more often than not.

Our transition from Oklahoma to Los Angeles was hard. Not just for all the obvious reasons of moving across the country, but because what was valued and where people found identity was so different in both places. In Oklahoma, relationships were grown over time with careful attention and value. You'd tend your friendships like a garden. And family? Well, family was everything.

In Los Angeles, relationships seemed more like currency. People often traded on who they knew and what a person could do for them. Rather than feeling as though I was a person worth knowing because I was loved, I often asked myself, *Do these people just want to know me because they want something from me? Are they hopeful I can get them to their next business opportunity or advance their career in some way?* It took an intentional effort to keep a trusting and open heart. I wanted to believe that people really did just want to know me for me.

The unfortunate truth is, I think we often treat God like He is someone we want to know because of what He can do for us. He's the guy who can get us to where we need to be next. He's got the inside scoop on our next steps, and we need to stay close to Him so we can have a good life.

I think it just might break God's heart when His children come to Him, hold out their hands, and then turn away, never getting to know His face. They want His favor, but not His friendship. They want His counsel, but not His companionship. They want His provision, but not His presence.

I'm not saying this is you or me all of the time. However, I am saying that we likely have both treated God this way at some point, and it is so important for us to acknowledge that there is more He is offering us. Because while He is a good dad who blesses us even when we're after His hands rather than

His heart, we miss the greater gift of what He is really offering us—Himself.

So, the question I asked in chapter 14 echoes here again: *What is it you really seek?*

Let's Pause and Ponder

If Jesus were to turn and ask you the question, "What do you seek?" what would you say? Why *do* you follow Him? Do you just want to know more about the life He offers you or what the Holy Spirit makes available to you? Or do you purely want to be with Him because you want to know Him as fully as you can? Be honest as you write your answer below.

_____

_____

_____

In your own words, what is the difference between knowing about Jesus and knowing Him? Why is it dangerous to replace our search for Him with information about Him?

_____

_____

_____

God So Close Chapter Questions

Just as we began our journey, let's revisit the same questions we pondered at the beginning, writing down who we know the Holy Spirit to be today.

Today, when I think of the Holy Spirit, I think of Him as . . .

_____

_____

When I think of the power God has given me, the first thing that comes to mind is . . .

_____

_____

Circle these True/False statements with your understanding today:

True or False   The Holy Spirit is a person.

True or False   The Holy Spirit speaks directly to Believers in Jesus today.

True or False   The Holy Spirit fills Believers today, supplying supernatural power and wisdom.

True or False   The Holy Spirit gives spiritual gifts to Believers today.

Let's Pray and Press In

Keep this in mind as we pray: There are no borders of the great expanse of God's being. And day by day, moment by moment, He is inviting us deeper into His heart.

Father God,

Thank You for sending Your Son, Jesus, and Your Holy Spirit so we can have a relationship with You. We have learned so much information through these last fourteen chapters, but more than facts, we have been reminded of the power of Your presence. We have spent time listening as You have taught and spoken to our hearts.

We acknowledge the Holy Spirit is God. We thank You for being as close as our breath. We are in awe of your holiness. We are humbled that you manifest Your presence in our midst. We thank You for the outpouring of Your Holy Spirit, who moves through us. We are grateful You haven't lost Your voice, and You help us discern when You are speaking. We will listen for the prompting and direction of Your Spirit. We will remember that You want to speak through us to others. We will yield to Your Spirit, who gives us gifts so that we can impact the world and help the body of Christ. And we will remember that You are the prize of all we seek. Thank You for leading us on this journey. Thank You for remaining God So Close. In Jesus' name we pray. Amen.

Take a moment to write out your own prayer. What do you want to tell God in this moment?

_____

_____

Listen as the Holy Spirit speaks right to your heart. What is His response? What is He reassuring you of now? Write below what you sense He is speaking to you now.

_____

_____

Let's continue to ask the Holy Spirit to continue to meet with us and explain to us spiritual things that foolish people cannot understand. Let's break free from the Enemy's lies about what God can't do. And let's go to His Word, looking at who the Holy Spirit reveals Himself to be and what our response to Him should look like. Let's bravely consider the power of a life awakened by His Spirit.

ABOUT THE AUTHOR

Becky Thompson is a bestselling author and the creator of the Midnight Mom Devotional community, where over one million moms gather online in nightly prayer. She and her husband, Jared, live in Northwest Oklahoma with their three children.

JOURNALING

_____

_____

_____

_____

_____

_____

_____

_____

_____

_____

_____

_____